# DR. DOORIDDLES

## A1

## Associative Reasoning Activities

**SERIES TITLES**
Dr. DooRiddles A1
Dr. DooRiddles B1
Dr. DooRiddles C1

## John H. Doolittle

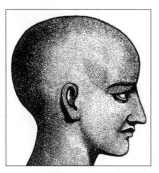

© 1991
**CRITICAL THINKING BOOKS & SOFTWARE**

www.CriticalThinking.com
(formerly Midwest Publications)
P.O. Box 448 • Pacific Grove • CA 93950-0448
Phone 800-458-4849 • FAX 831-393-3277
ISBN 0-89455-437-9
Printed in the United States of America

## ABOUT THE AUTHOR

John Doolittle has been a professor of psychology at California State University, Sacramento since 1966. He received a bachelor's degree in biology and psychology from Stanford University, a master's degree in psychology from San Jose State University, and a doctoral degree in experimental psychology from the University of Colorado, Boulder. At Sacramento, Dr. Doolittle has taught in the schools of Education, Arts and Sciences, and Engineering and Computer Science. He has also been a visiting professor at the University of Melbourne, Australia. Dr. Doolittle is author or coauthor of a number of books and software published by Critical Thinking Books & Software, including *Riddle Mysteries* software, three volumes of *Dr. DooRiddles*, and *Creative Problem Solving Activities A1, B1,* and *C1*.

# TEACHER SUGGESTIONS

Everyone loves the mystery of a riddle and Dr. DooRiddles will bring laughter, groans, and challenges (perhaps for as much as a week or more per riddle) to you and your students.

## Thinking Skills

Perceiving relationships between words, ideas, and concepts is called associative reasoning, which is a skill necessary for creative thought. Riddle solving requires students to use important skills of associative, inductive, and divergent thinking to find the answers. Students will learn to recognize important ideas, examine these ideas from different points of view, and then find connections between the ideas. These teachable skills are essential for efficient, successful, open-ended problem solving of all kinds.

## Role of the Student

Although Dr. DooRiddles are fun and tantalizing, answering them is not simple play. In order to solve these riddles, students have to generate solutions in many different categories. Students often confuse multiple-category generation of answers with offering the same answer rephrased. To clarify this confusion, students need to learn how to examine an idea from many reference points.

For example:

> If one of the given clues in a riddle were the word *horn*, students would have to think of different meanings and applications of that word. Does it refer to a kind of musical instrument? a part of an animal? to the geographic term? a general horn shape? or does it refer to an alternative in a dilemma?

## Role of the Teacher

At first, the teacher will need to help students learn how to produce multiple-category solutions by asking higher level thinking questions. Eventually, responsibility of self-questioning should be turned over to the students. Teach your students to ask themselves questions such as: How is the clue used? Why is it phrased this way? Is this clue connected to a clue in another line? How else can this word be spelled? Is this a whole word or a partial word? Does this line mean what it says or is it a play on words? Does this word sound like another word?

Students should be encouraged to "listen" to the riddles, examining the sound of each line and individual words, and to use visual imagery to "see" what's happening. As they get into the process of riddle solving, they will learn to read and weigh the importance of each word in each line so they can interpret the clues correctly. They will learn to notice how highly descriptive adjectives, verbs, and adverbs indicate specific kinds of movement or action; and how unusual phonetic spellings, homonyms, prefixes, suffixes, roots, puns, analogies, and multiple word meanings are used to both hide and reveal the clues.

Always ask students why they chose the answer they did. Do not allow students to just give their answer without explaining the reasoning behind it. When answers are backed up and evaluated in group discussions, class members share their knowledge, connect it to other ideas and explore the concept in many directions to find a "best" answer from among possible multiple answers. By working and sharing information in groups, children who are not familiar with the culture, or who lack English proficiency, will expand their knowledge, build more extensive vocabulary, and will be able to apply information more diversely.

## Classroom Application

These materials make great sponge activities and are excellent activities for independent, cooperative, or open learning situations. The riddles can be used as part of the daily thinking skill curriculum or for the challenge of the week. The riddles spiral up in difficulty within each book and from level to level so that teachers may select the appropriate level of difficulty for students.

Dr. DooRiddles cuts across curriculum areas and deals with real-world objects and situations. Both teachers and students will find the mind-broadening strategies used in these challenging activities richly rewarding at test-taking time.

# ANSWERS

**Page 1**
cat
book
blue

**Page 2**
apple
car
pig

**Page 3**
red
dog
lemon

**Page 4**
toe
cow
train

**Page 5**
tiger
yellow
boat

**Page 6**
duck
goose
green

**Page 7**
goat
cherry
camel

**Page 8**
donkey
bear
rooster

**Page 9**
nose
rabbit
grapes

**Page 10**
lion
wolf
squirrel

**Page 11**
orange
owl
pencil

**Page 12**
peach
horse
paper

**Page 13**
shoes
zebra
belt

**Page 14**
eagle
giraffe
coyote

**Page 15**
backpack
run
rat

**Page 16**
violet
bicycle
snow

**Page 17**
jump
ear
kick

**Page 18**
hen or chicken
lawn
throw or toss

**Page 19**
skates
airplane
neck

**Page 20**
hit
eye
finger

**Page 21**
banana
dig
rain

**Page 22**
fog
spaghetti
wind

**Page 23**
nickel
inch
oil

**Page 24**
mile
sandwich
wood

**Page 25**
glass
quarter
taco

**Page 26**
uncle
penguin
gold

**Page 27**
pie
bus
saw

**Page 28**
warm or cool
pop
cousin

**Page 29**
pelican
gallon
sister

**Page 30**
pound
steel
teaspoon

**Page 31**
shoot or shot
turtle
cute

**Page 32**
ugly
juice
hail

**Page 33**
fair
stew
pizza

**Page 34**
quart
silver
damp

**Page 35**
mother
heart
seven

**Page 36**
shadow
storm
**round** table, **round**s

**Page 37**
Old **North** Church, **north**
Captain **Hook**, **hook**
tooth

**Page 38**
Peter **Pumpkin**eater, **pumpkin**
flag
weeds

**Page 39**
dirt
wrong
pants

**Page 40**
**win**ter, **win**ner
**wag**on, **wag**
riddle

# MODEL LESSON

*My tail can wag,*
*My feet there are four;*
*I scratch or bark,*
*When I want out the door.*

Each line, or pair of lines, in the above riddle contains a clue to the answer. Carefully read each line and try to figure out what is being described. Look for clue words. Try to form a picture in your mind as you connect all the clues. Ask yourself questions about each of the clues.

For Example:

In the first line, *tail* and *wag* are clue words.  What has a tail and wags it?

In the second line, *four feet* are clue words. What has four feet? and a tail that can wag?

In the third line, *scratch* and *bark* are clue words. What scratches and barks?

In the fourth line, *want out the door* goes with scratch and bark. What scratches and barks when it wants out the door?

Now how would you connect all the clues? Perhaps the first thing that comes to mind as an answer is a dog. Let's see if dog works. A dog does have a tail, and it wags it when it is happy. A dog does have four feet. When a dog wants to go out, it often scratches or barks to let its owner know. So *dog* does fit all the clues and it is a good answer.

Someone else may come up with a different answer, and if it fits all the clues, it is also a good answer.

I will chase a mouse,
And I start with C;
I will chase a bird
And I end with T.

*What am I?* .........................

I have many pages,
And I start with a B;
Before you learned to read,
Someone read to you from me.

*What am I?* .........................

The color of the sky,
And I start with B;
And if it's deep and clear,
The lake is colored me.

*What am I?* .........................

A fruit of red or green,
And I start with an A;
My juice is brown and sweet,
My core you throw away.

*What am I?* ........................

You take me for a drive,
And I start with C;
But if I'm out of fuel,
You won't ride in me.

*What am I?* ........................

I just love the mud,
And I start with P;
I am fat and smart,
And I end with G.

*What am I?* ........................

My color means please stop,
And I end in D;
And some fire engines,
Have been painted me.

*What am I?* .........................

I will be your friend,
And I start with D;
I will guard your house,
And I end with G.

*What am I?* .........................

A very sour fruit,
And I start with L;
Add water and sugar,
And I taste just swell.

*What am I?* .........................

I'm down near the ground,
And I start with a T;
I'm part of a foot,
Folks call me piggie.

*What am I?* ........................

I eat lots of grass,
And I start with C;
The milk in your lunch,
All began with me.

*What am I?* ........................

I start with T,
That's my railroad;
I may say, "Choo!,"
And not have a cold.

*What am I?* ........................

I live in the jungle,
And I start with T;
I have stripes and sharp teeth,
My middle letter's G.

*What am I?* ........................

The color of the sun,
And I start with Y;
There are two L's in me,
Guess me, oh please try.

*What am I?* ........................

I ride on the water,
And I start with B;
With sail or motor,
You can go with me.

*What am I?* ........................

My sound is a quack,
And I start with D;
I can fly or swim,
It is up to me.

*What am I?* .........................

I have a large bill,
And I start with G;
I've a long, white neck,
And I end with E.

*What am I?* .........................

The color of a tree,
And I start with a G;
And if you have a lawn,
Let's hope it's colored me.

*What am I?* .........................

I will chew on a can,
And I start with G;
I will chew on grass,
And I end with T.

*What am I?* ........................

---

I'm a little, red fruit,
And I start with C;
George Washington with axe,
Once chopped down my tree.

*What am I?* ........................

---

I live on the desert,
And I start with C;
I have one or two humps,
So, don't look for three.

*What am I?* ........................

You may call me burro,
And I start with D;
Put a load on my back,
You can count on me.

*What am I?* ........................

---

I sleep through the winter,
And I start with B;
When you're in the state parks,
Please, please don't feed me.

*What am I?* ........................

---

Cock-a-doodle-doo,
And I start with R;
I crow at the sun,
And I end with R.

*What am I?* ........................

I stick out of your face,
And I end with an E;
But if you have a cold,
You won't smell much with me.

*What am I?* ........................

I love to eat carrots,
And I end with a T;
I'm so soft and fluffy,
You love to cuddle me.

*What am I?* ........................

A fruit of red or green,
And I start with a G;
You'll find me on a vine,
With more bunches like me.

*What am I?* ........................

My wife does all the hunting,
While I just lie around;
My loud roar tells you I'm king,
My mane looks like a crown.

*What am I?* ........................

Across the frozen North,
I hunt with my pack;
We're searching for a herd,
That we can track.

*What am I?* ........................

I will gather some nuts,
And I start with S;
See my bushy tail,
Am I hard to guess?

*What am I?* ........................

The color of a juice,
And I end with E;
A fruit that is quite sweet,
Is named for me.

*What am I?* ........................

See me in the tree,
I do give a hoot;
I'm looking for mice,
My big eyes are cute.

*What am I?* ........................

I can be very sharp,
And I start with P;
You can even erase,
What you wrote with me.

*What am I?* ........................

I'm a fuzzy, sweet fruit,
And I start with a P;
A pit is what is left,
When you're done eating me.

*What am I?* .........................

I pulled the stagecoach,
And I end with E;
It takes a blacksmith,
To put shoes on me.

*What am I?* .........................

I'm what you write upon,
And I start with P;
If you fold me just right,
Then you can fly me.

*What am I?* .........................

        © 1991 MIDWEST PUBLICATIONS / CRITICAL THINKING PRESS & SOFTWARE • P.O. Box 448, Pacific Grove, CA 93950

I start and end with S,
And your feet I hide;
Rub me on the mat,
If you've been outside.

*What am I?* .........................

---

I have many stripes,
And I start with Z;
I am black and white,
Surely you've seen me.

*What am I?* .........................

---

I can hold up pants,
And I start with B;
As you start to grow,
You change the notch on me.

*What am I?* .........................

I am a large bird,
I start and end with E;
My nest is very high,
That soaring bird is me.

*What am I?* ........................

My neck is so long,
And I start with G;
I eat leaves in trees,
There's an R in me.

*What am I?* ........................

I look like a wild dog,
And I start with C;
I yap and howl at night,
And I end with E.

*What am I?* ........................

**14**

I ride on your shoulders,
And I start with B;
And I carry your books,
Your lunch rides in me.

*What am I?* .........................

I mean to go fast,
And I start with R;
Of course you could walk,
And go just as far.

*What am I?* .........................

I love to eat cheese,
And I end with T;
I have a long tail,
A cat's chasing me!

*What am I?* .........................

A color like purple,
And I start with V;
I am very pretty,
And I end with T.

*What am I?* .........................

I have two wheels,
And I start with B;
Unless I'm training,
Then see four on me.

*What am I?* .........................

We're a bunch of flakes,
Whose name starts with S;
Think of white winters,
And maybe you'll guess.

*What am I?* .........................

   © 1991 MIDWEST PUBLICATIONS / CRITICAL THINKING PRESS & SOFTWARE • P.O. Box 448, Pacific Grove, CA 93950

I mean to go high,
And I start with J;
See me go over,
The thing in my way.

*What am I?* ........................

I catch all the sounds,
And I start with E;
I look like a shell,
You see by the sea.

*What am I?* ........................

I'm done with the foot,
And I start with K;
The ball comes to me,
I send it away.

*What am I?* ........................

I will lay an egg,
And I eat corn from the ground;
And with my sisters,
I make a clucking sound.

*What am I?* ........................

I start with L,
And I rhyme with dawn;
I'm thick and green,
And fun to play on.

*What am I?* ........................

I'm done with the arm,
And I start with T;
If you want to pitch,
Then you must do me.

*What am I?* ........................

Wheels on your feet,
Blades if there is ice;
I begin with S,
Falling isn't nice.

*What am I?* ........................


I fly through the air,
And I start with A;
Fasten your seat belt,
And we're on our way.

*What am I?* ........................


I sit upon your shoulders,
And I end with K;
You would surely lose your head,
If I went away.

*What am I?* ........................

I'm done with a bat,
And I end with T;
To get a home run,
Then you must do me.

*What am I?* ........................

I look out on the world,
And I start with E;
You would depend on hearing,
If it weren't for me.

*What am I?* ........................

I start with an F,
Which doesn't stand for fail;
The part of your hand,
That ends up in a nail.

*What am I?* ........................

I'm a yellow fruit,
And I start with B;
You could fall right down,
If you stepped on me.

*What am I?* .........................

I'm how you make a hole,
And I start with D;
You may need a shovel,
And I end with G.

*What am I?* .........................

I'm a source of water,
And I contain an A;
If I'm in the forecast,
You'll stay inside to play.

*What am I?* .........................

I'm a very thick mist,
And I contain a G;
You may see me in London,
Or out upon the sea.

*What am I?* ........................

A noodle dish from Italy,
That's very hard to spell;
I start with S and end with I,
Please ring the dinner bell.

*What am I?* ........................

I contain an N,
I'm air that's on the move;
I can bend a tree,
And all its leaves remove.

*What am I?* ........................

Think now of a coin,
That's less than a dime;
More than a penny,
Can you guess what I'm?

*What am I?* ........................

---

A measure of length,
And I rhyme with pinch;
I'm less than a foot,
This should be a cinch.

*What am I?* ........................

---

From black pools in the earth,
I'm pumped up from a well;
They put me in tankers,
And hope that I don't spill.

*What am I?* ........................

I'm how far you drove the car,
And I rhyme with style;
I am longer than a foot,
Guess me and you'll smile.


*What am I?* ........................


Two pieces of bread,
A food for your lunch;
You choose what goes in,
And then start to munch.


*What am I?* ........................


I come from the forest,
And I contain a D;
Sometimes in the winter,
You may set fire to me.


*What am I?* ........................

I am really brittle,
And I contain an L;
You can see right through me,
What am I? Can you tell?

*What am I?* ........................

A coin called two bits,
That's less than a dollar;
Or think of a fourth,
Now guess me, you scholar.

*What am I?* ........................

A folded corn tortilla,
You fill with cheese and meat;
Now add lettuce and sauce,
And you have a tasty treat.

*What am I?* ........................

A brother to your parent,
And I contain a C;
I'm married to your nice aunt,
I hope that you guess me.

*What am I?* .........................

I'm a bird who walks or swims,
But who cannot fly;
My eggs are on the land,
That by the sea does lie.

*What am I?* .........................

I'm a shiny metal,
And I end with a D;
Look at your good jewelry,
And you may well see me.

*What am I?* .........................

I am a good dessert,
And I start with P;
And I do rhyme with fly,
Can't you just taste me?

*What am I?* ........................

Some kids will ride me,
To get to their school;
Mostly painted yellow,
I'm no horse or mule.

*What am I?* ........................

I must cut the wood,
And I start with S;
I rhyme with paw,
Now, then, can you guess?

*What am I?* ........................

I am not cold,
I am not hot;
With these two gone,
What else have you got?

*What am I?* ........................

I'm a name for your dad,
And I rhyme with mop;
I'm a name for soda,
Push tab or screw top.

*What am I?* ........................

Child of your aunt,
And I contain a U;
First, second or step,
Ah well, how do you do?

*What am I?* ........................

A sea bird with a long bill,
I dive to get my food;
And I rhyme with "Well, he can..."
Now, can you guess me, dude?

*What am I?* ........................

I'm a unit of gas,
You pay for what is pumped;
And I contain an A,
I hope that you're not stumped.

*What am I?* ........................

I contain an S,
And I contain a T;
Think now of a girl,
That is in the family.

*What am I?* ........................

I'm a unit of weight,
I'm a thing hammers do;
Scales tell how many,
There are of me in you.

*What am I?* ........................

I'm very hard and shiny,
And I contain a T;
Bridges and ships and tow trucks,
Are all made out of me.

*What am I?* ........................

I'm a unit of sugar,
You add to your iced tea;
And I am eight letters long,
A cup is more than me.

*What am I?* ........................

I'm done with a ball,
And I start with S;
I go in a hoop,
I hope you can guess.

*What am I?* ........................

Please check out my shell,
I'm slow and I'm green;
I walk on the land,
Or go submarine.

*What am I?* ........................

I'm adorable,
In every way;
And I rhyme with boot,
Or so they all say.

*What am I?* ........................

Now I am just not pretty,
And I contain a G;
But like the famous duckling,
You have to wait and see.

*What am I?* ........................

I'm orange and in a glass,
Upon a breakfast table;
And I do rhyme with Bruce,
But I don't rhyme with Mabel.

*What am I?* ........................

I'm hard, icy balls,
That hurt if they hit you;
And I start with H,
Now, what does that get you?

*What am I?* ........................

I'm very nice weather,
And I rhyme with air;
The day is so pleasant,
I don't have a care.

*What am I?* .........................

A dish with chunks of meat,
And gravy very brown;
And I contain an E,
So when do we sit down?

*What am I?* .........................

I'm baked in an oven,
But I am not a cake;
There're Z's in my name,
What a meal I make.

*What am I?* .........................

I'm a measure of milk,
And I contain a U;
I'm larger than a cup,
There's an A in me too.

*What am I?* ........................

I am mined from the ground,
And I do contain an ER;
I used to be in dollars,
That weren't made out of paper.

*What am I?* ........................

A word that means moist,
I'm somewhat less than wet;
I start with a D,
Have you thought of me yet?

*What am I?* ........................

For nine months I was your home,
And I contain a T;
Such a very special day,
Is set aside for me.

*What am I?* ........................

---

I'm the thing that thumps,
When you've been on a run;
I'm on Valentines,
That you send just for fun.

*What am I?* ........................

---

Think first of a number,
Called lucky by some;
Or think of four and three,
Now, what do they sum?

*What am I?* ........................

All day I do follow,
Each move you have made;
When I'm cast by a tree,
Then I am called shade.

*What am I?* ........................

High winds and rain,
Or sleet and snow;
Call the small boats,
Tell them, "Don't go!"

*What am I?* ........................

My table held the food,
For Arthur and the knights;
Or else I tell how long,
They've lasted in the fight.

*What am I?* ........................

From my old church steeple,
It was two if by sea;
Or go my direction,
Old Santa for to see.

*What am I?* ........................

My Captain is the one,
Who battled Peter Pan;
I'm the end of the line,
For that worm in the can.

*What am I?* ........................

From out of your mouth I do pop,
And with truth I do rhyme;
Under your pillow I'll become,
A coin during night time.

*What am I?* ........................

My eater was a man,
I think his name was Peter;
Or cut a face in me,
And I'm a scary greeter.

*What am I?* ........................

I wave every day,
Without going away;
You give me your pledge,
To start off the school day.

*What am I?* ........................

We grow in the garden,
But we weren't invited;
So we are pulled or sprayed,
Whenever we're sighted.

*What am I?* ........................

I'm not hamburger,
And yet I am ground;
And I rhyme with Bert,
On kids' clothes I'm found.

*What am I?* ........................

Though I contain a W,
It doesn't make a sound;
My fate is never to be right,
This poem is quite profound.

*What am I?* ........................

Think of a tired dog,
Who's run around the block;
Or think of what to wear,
That starts about the socks.

*What am I?* ........................

With ter I can be cold,
The trees are damp with snow;
With ner it was my race,
To best the rest, you know.

*What am I?* ........................

My gun just cannot shoot,
But rolls on four wheels;
Alone my dog's tail,
Tells just how good he feels.

*What am I?* ........................

A four-line poem,
Surprise and delight;
Which only happens,
When you get it right.

*What am I?* ........................

© 1991 MIDWEST PUBLICATIONS / CRITICAL THINKING PRESS & SOFTWARE • P.O. Box 448, Pacific Grove, CA 93950